start your own business & make it successful.
In the harsh reality, where nobody cares

start your own business & make it successful.
In the harsh reality, where nobody cares

Jasmin Hajro

Jasmin Hajro

© 2020 Jasmin Hajro

Cover design by Jasmin Hajro

Jasmin Hajro

First edition 2020

In this book you will discover:

The bio of entrepreneur & author Jasmin Hajro

&

book start your own business and make it successful.
In the harsh reality, where nobody cares

&

book Recipe for Happiness

&

A small introduction to establishment Hajro

The bio of entrepreneur & author Jasmin Hajro,
get acquainted ...

Hello dear reader, how are you ?

Thank you for purchasing this book.

My name is Jasmin Hajro, I was born on July 6, 1985 in Bosnia.

We came to the Netherlands as refugees 21 years ago.

After finishing school & several jobs ...

On December 17, 2012, I founded my first company: investment company Jasko.

After a successful first year, I unfortunately had to close the company.

After a short period of rest, unemployment benefits

and temporary work. I started as an entrepreneur again.

On September 1, 2015, I founded the company Hajro.

Since the beginning, the core business is, selling sets or packages of greeting cards, door to door.

Today the product range has expanded.

With the selling of my 45 books such as:

book Moneymaker &

book Build your fortune.

Part of the Royalties from my books are donated to the Charity.

My company has a few subsidiaries, like Hajro Franchise and Hajro Consulting...

For more information about my company , go to www.hajro-international.webnode.nl

Hello dear stubborn one,
how are you ?

Yes, if you want to start your own business,
and want to do business ...

Then you are probably a bit stubborn.
And that is good.
Things should go your way
the way you want.

Because it is your life.
You probably can't stand it if others tell you what to do.
And that is good.
You should rule.
Because it is your life.

Today is Wednesday,

if it is good.

Actually it is already Thursday, because it's already been midnight, half an hour ago.

To be honest, I woke up a little later this afternoon.

Around 1pm and before I left for work I felt like I was about to die.

Nevertheless, I went anyway and made 4 sales.

A sale is when someone buys a product from me.

If someone buys a gift mug from me for 5 euros, then that is 1 sale.

What can you learn from this?

First, there will be days when you just feel like shit.

It really sucks like you've been drinking the night before.

But you don't even drink & just feel like shit.

Then you discipline yourself & do what you have to do:

Go to work and earn money.

If I didn't went out to work,

I wouldn't have earned anything..

What can you expect from this book?
I never claimed to be successful but I am.
Because I made sales every month,
every month, 3 years in a row.
And we measure success with earned dollars.
I best just be honest with you.
Tell you honestly how I started my business
& how i'm making it successful.
You can then learn from my experience,
what things you shouldn't do,
which you should do,
and what you should do more of.

Because,

the usual recipe for starting and running your own business is:

you have an idea,

you want to work for yourself,

you register with the Chamber of Commerce,

you create your website,

you write your Business Plan.

You go to the bank with your business plan,

convinces the consultant

(who knows little about entrepreneurship because he is an employee of the bank)

and you are funded.

You get 10 or 20 thousand euros or dollars,

to make your dream come true.

And you are going to do business.

I started my first company in December 2012.
Called Jasko.
I had a hard time finding work in that era, and if I could find something it probably would are production work (manual labor jobs).
I didn't want to do that for the rest of my life.
And I loved finance and investing ,
so I started my own investment business.
Before that I had taken courses, read books and invested as a private individual.
So I could also do it for other people.
I also had a financial system to use for it.
I currently have a patent for that financial system.
I've done all those things which I had described above with the usual recipe for business.
But I did not get a loan from the bank.
I made my own flyers and delivered them myself.
And I invested my own money first in the portfolio.
After that I found 4 more customers who invested.
My Mom, dad, my sister and my ex girlfriend.
At most, there was 1,600 euros in the portfolio (the wallet)

I did pay out a 10% return in the first year.

But a 10% return on 1600, - euros is 160, - in profit.

Of Which I had to pay out a part to my investors.

I couldn't live on that.

I've held it stubbornly for a long time …

almost 3 years.

I also delivered brochures to earn extra.

I started Hajro Chores,

to do household chores for people for a fee.

And I worked at Rabelink for a while as a loader / unloader.

In the end I deregistered at the Chamber of Commerce, with pain in my heart.

I was very sad.

What can you learn from this?

Some people may not believe in your company, friends and family of yours too.

And neither does the bank.

Do you think if I could sell better that I would have had more investors?

I'm sure I would.

Because whether you have an idea (such as insurance or investment),

a service (taking care of administration)

or product (gift mugs).

You have to be able to sell it to people.
So that they become your customers and you earn money because of what you give them in exchange or what you do for them.
It's not the end of the world even though it felt like it then.

I got the chance to start selling greeting cards on behalf of a foundation.
And that would be good training
to prepare me as an energy consultant .
Because in sales, you always have work.
So I also registered again at the Chamber of Commerce, on September 1, 2015, my second business called Hajro.
And I kept selling sets of greeting cards on behalf of that foundation.
And I made money ,I was paid for it.
Many people were much nicer than I expected when I went out selling, door to door.

I did have sales training before that.
Because the partners of that foundation broke up,
I went to the notary and founded a new foundation,
with the earnings of my greetingcard sales...
I called it : the Giveth Life foundation.
Then there was some hassle with the police about
needing a permit to collect on behalf of the
foundation.
You will receive a permit for 2 weeks per year to be
able to collect in the municipality of Doetinchem.
That was of little use to me.
So I went on
selling packages of greetingcards on behalf of my
company Hajro
. That's called peddling and you can do without a
permit.
And I still do.
Like today, out which.... at the beginning of this book
I told you about .

And maybe it was also time for a new book.
What do you think ?
It is only my 14th book.

(You will soon learn in the book Double your Profits,

also to start writing and selfpublishing your books.

So that you and your company become better known,

you help people by sharing information,

and you can earn something from it.)

In the beginning I learned the most important thing of entrepreneurship.

That is SELLING.

Because even though you're a carpenter

you have to sell to a human first that you are the

right person to get that job done.

Only then can you do your craft (the carpentry).

Because of the sales that you make,

money enters your company.

As Zig Ziglar says:

"Only selling contributes to profit, everything else contributes to cost."

But yah, I was also very opinionated.

And I wanted a big, beautiful grand internet shop.

And I had to have something in case the greeting cards would sell less well.

Because the new generation is less traditional, than

the old generation.
For the old generation it's normal to send a greetingcard.
At least for birthdays and for Christmas & New Year.
So I needed a different product that I could easily take with me and that people often use.

That became the gift mug, because people keep drinking their coffee or tea drink from a mug.
And it's wrapped like a present so you can also give it as a present.
Problem solved.
So I went on to build my grandiose online shop.
Oh yeah....
So I had ordered 1000 mugs, 1000 pens and 1000 lighters with my companys logo on them.
With payment afterwards, while I didn't have the money for it then.
I thought, I just keep selling and pay them in installments a little every month.
But that supplier thought it took a long time,
hired an aggressive debt collection agency, that wanted to declare me bankrupt and the amount I had to pay doubled.
That sucked.

I was furious at that debt collector,

but it was my fault.

I was responsible.

Well you won't believe it but I was saved by the Tax Office. (the Dutch IRS)

I got some money back a few times, and paid that supplier.

Saved by the tax authorities.

I also have sets of greeting cards to sell,

for birthdays & at the end of the year greeting cards for Christmas & New Year.

So I still have some boxes with mugs,

but sales are going well.

People buy every month a number of gift cups, as we call them.

So I proceeded to build my grandiose online shop.

With Greeting cards for different occasions,

with different themes.

Printed clothing,

laptops from china,

beauty sets,

health sets,

greeting card subscriptions.

It was never finished ….
every time I still had to do something on it…
change some more, make another improvement.
During that period I earned less,
because I was more behind the computer then
in the field chasing after customers.
Well when I finally got it done I had not paid my
website subscription for a month.
My site went offline, and someone bought my
domain: www.hajro.nl
That is also printed on my flyers and business cards.
That was really shit.
It takes time and money and energy
, to create a new website and have new flyers and
business cards printed.
I made some temporary free websites, and eventually
the website at www.mijndomein.nl
which we still have.
And which, thank God, is doing well.
Of course it has become www.hajrobv.nl
It's less extensive than it used to be,
anyway I decided to use only Hajro products to sell.
And no aloe vera and other stuff from other people.
As a company, we have donated since the beginning

to 20 Charities.

It is our responsibility to contribute to a better region.
That is why we do not ask for anything back for our donations.
And today we support more than 40 Charities.
And you too, by buying this book.
Thanks.

It is now almost 2 o'clock at night.
And I'm writing a book that you are reading now.
You might find that strange or weird.
You can respect it too.
You will learn later too to keep on working.
To make long days.
To start over.
To work 6 days in a row.

To work 7 days in a row,
even 7 days a week...

I want a great internet shop or online store after all
such as Amazon.com and Bol.com and many people
who order from me.
But I've only had 2 orders, in the past 3 years.
My former friends and my family can still order
something small from me, right?
But that did not happen.
You will be disappointed.
And that feels like shit or fucked or whatever you
describe it when you are fed up and disappointed
and experiencing negative emotions.
But as Jim Rohn says:
"Learn to discipline your disappointments."
So you ain't gonna cry about it but persevere.
I have already described 3 times how shitty and shit
it was.
I don't want to discourage you.
I want The opposite.
You have to start your own business
and and I think you can.
I think you can make it successful.
As the title of this book indicates,

this is about starting your own business and making it successful, in the harsh reality.

In the beginning you will earn little ...

or at least less than your last-earned salary.

You will have to keep going

continue to believe in yourself and what you do.

Especially persevere.

In January 2016 I had made 9 sales.

That is EUR 45 in profit

45, - euros in income throughout the month.

What would you do?

In the next month?

Well I persisted.

In February 2016

I had 25 sales and received 100 euros,

that is a total of 225 euros in income for the entire month.

What would you do the next month?

Look for other work .....

Do something else?

I persisted.

Last month,

September 2018

I had 103 sales x 5 = E 515,- in profits

plus 37, - euro royalties from my books.

A total of 552 euros

What would you have done the month after?

I keep going and you will soon do that too.

I'm gonna double the time that I'm selling then I also double my sales and therefore my profit and income.

If I've made 103 sales by 4 hours a day to work,

so half days.

That is 5 days times 4 hours is 20 hours a week,

that is times 4 weeks so 80 hours in a month.

In 80 hours of selling, I made 103 sales.

And earned 515 euros.

So if I double my selling time to 8 hours a day.

That is 40 hour a week and 160 hours per month,

then I make 206 sales and about 1030 euros in profit.

Then I can sell 180 hours a month to earn even more.

And the more I study

(yes I read books about selling & you will too.

It is Required for success)

and the more people I speak to and the more experience I get get with selling.

The more sales I make.

To eventually build a team of salespeople,

to increase sales & profits tenfold. Or a hundredfold.

Because we live in reality some wrong people will want to take your money away.
So replace the locks on your front door and your back door.
Buy 2 cameras, one to keep an eye on your front door and one to keep an eye on your back door.
Buy good internet security such as Kaspersky or Bitdefender, with an extra module for safe internet shopping and safe internet banking.
A number of people will believe in you and always there for you.
You can often count them on 1 hand.
Because you have 5 fingers on 1 hand.
You'll have about 5 supporters.
Your dad can do that, mother, brother or sister and someone else.
Cherish these golden people.
Show appreciation and give them money and presents.

Because the rest of the world doesn't care much if you had anything to eat today.

I've already passed the breakeven point.
When you have more profit than costs.
But it took about 3 years.
Well now that you know that,
you can be prepared for it.
And keep going.
Whatever they say to you.
If you have little holes in your fingertips,
and don't feel good ….
. Report this to the police.
Those are ways
, how wrong people try to steal your money.
Hopefully that bit on security helps,
to prevent things like that.
Even though there are lows and tough times,
doing business is great. And having your own business
and lifetime emplyment is great.
You have freedom.
And selling is the best profession that there is.
The feeling when you make a sale is awesome.
And your customer with your product in the hands and
a big smile on the face is really great.
And especially because you support Charities together

and do something good.

You see, it is much more than selling a package of greetingcards or a mug.

To be continued.

Are you looking forward to the 2nd part?

By now, the time that I am translating this book,

that I wrote about 2 years ago….

I have some notes and extra's to add…

It is now Sunday january 10th 2021,

we are in corona crisis for about a year…

And the Netherlands is in national lockdown.

To continue working I ordered thousands of flyers,

made another online store with more than 100 different greetingcards….

And I started selling loafs of bread and bottles of carbon water

along with my packages of greetingcards,

to be able to continue sellling…

Bread and water are essential…

The whole point of this book is to show how it really is

in reality

to start your own business…

It's tough and challenging,

as you've already read….

I will add 2 short stories or articles that I wrote on

www.medium.com

And I will add 2 booklets of mine,

to help you on your entrepreneurial journey...

I would like to give you a booklet as a gift,
you can read it on the following pages…
It will help you to be more relaxed,
If you are relaxed,
you will be more productive and
make more sales and profits.

The Recipe for Happiness, introduction

A book has been written about a true story ...
About a man who was imprisoned in a concentration camp
at the time of Hitler,
and happy.

So,
Happiness has nothing to do with your circumstances.

It has everything to do with,
your choice to be happy,
regardless of circumstances.

Choose to be happy.

Of course there are touhger times in life,
like when someone you love,
dies.
That's part of life.
Those times of grief you just have to go through and process.

Processing is best done by talking about it,
to get it off your chest regularly.

Or by writing about it,

if you write down a situation or your feelings about it,
then it's on paper,
and it is less in your head.
Writing is a good outlet.

Processing is also done well by:
staying busy.
Whether that is in your work or your hobby.
They say: a rolling stone does not collect moss.

So stay busy ....

Okay, now you have learned a good lesson about how to
better process negative life experiences.

But you're here for the Recipe for Happiness, right?

Well, the lesson you've learned will help to
make the recipe work better for you.

Chapter I

Here it comes then ...

You have probably read a local newspaper,
and you regularly check the news.

(the daily news on television)

Have you noticed that about 99% of it is bad news?
Only misery ..
If you did not know better,
you would think that the whole world is going to perish.

If it's a habit for you,
to watch the news every day for half an hour ...

Have you ever wondered if it's healthy for you?
Does it make you happy ?

Of course not !

The easiest way to change a habit is
by replacing it with a new habit.

So from today on,
instead of watching the worldly news
half an hour a day ....

Watch COMEDY for half an hour a day.

Mandatory.

Every day.

Well, now at half past eight in the evening it's not news time,
but Comedy time.

If you watch comedy,
you relax &
you laugh.

Sounds healthier, doesn't it?

Well, laughing every day is easy to do, right?

And replacing your old bad habit in this way,
with a nice, healthy new habit,
is probably easier than you thought.

Except that relaxation is good for you,
when you laugh,
your body makes endorphins.

Those are natural happiness substances.

Well, after 21 days of daily watching comedy,
you will have formed a new habit.

So watch Comedy every day.

You can watch a lot of standup comedy on Youtube for free.

Simple?
Sure, but you have to do it,
every day,
until you don't have to think about it anymore,
and you start doing it automatically.

Chapter II

Some Happiness Ingredients in a row:

- Watch comedy every day, at least one hour.

- Eat ice cream, treat someone with an ice cream.

- Work out, throw out your frustration by playing tennis or go for a run.

— Pee in the yard
(and if you get a fine for urinating, laugh your ass off)

— Do not worry, life is too short for that
(by staying busy, you do not have time to worry)

— Hug the people that you love

— Go enjoy a cup of coffee or tea

— Buy or save a cat or some other pet

- When you receive money, immediately save a part of it

- Don't let the media scare you,
the world is not getting worse, the world is getting better.

- Sex, need I say more
(when you have sex your body also produces endorphins =
those natural happiness substances)

Maybe the Recipe for Happiness

is different than you had expected....

But that doesn't matter,

the point is that it works &

that it will help you to live happier.

Do it,

it is easier

then looking with a sour face.

Note from the author

If you liked this book & got some value from it.

Would you then be so kind,

please,

to recommend it

to the people that you know.

So that they too can enjoy it

and live happier.

Thank you very much.

_____

It was my pleasure to write and translate

this book (my third one) for you.

I hope it helps you to live happier.

(I know it will, if you do the things it teaches)

And I hope, that we can together make a contribution

to more happiness in the world.

We can.
If you recommend this book
and share it.
Then I will promote it.

And together we will make a contribution to

a happier world.

I would appreciate it if you would write a short review.
Thank you for your effort.

Kind regards,

Jasmin Hajro

*the Ultimate Winning Strtagey
for entrepreneurs and salespeople,*

you can read on the following pages

" By the way, I started my first company in 2012.

I have made more than 700 sales since

1 September 2015 so far.

So I have a track record
in sales and business,
and I know what I'm talking about. "

"" As you have probably already understood,
I earn my money by selling for my own company.
That's my work.

The proceeds from my books go to charity.

I write from experience,
I write to help people move forward
in their lives and business "

The Ultimate Winning Strategy for entrepreneurs

How do we measure success in business?
With monetary points, with earned euro's or dollars.

What is a successful business?

Successful entrepreneurship =
selling a lot

We are therefore successfully running our business,
if we sell a lot.

So success in doing business = selling a lot
(many sales realized / many sales closed)

Because sales means profits.

So what is the Ultimate Winning Strategy in business?

First we start with the concept,
then you get 2 examples from real life

Have you noticed that supermarkets are open 7 days a week?

Supermarkets may be a less good example,
because we just have to eat and drink.

Have you been to the Esso gas station?
(Part of Exxon mobil corporation)
The Esso gas station has a shop with staff,
and is open 24 hours a day, 7 days a week.

And no, even if it seems that we need petrol,
the Esso could also have become a self-service gas station,
where you fill your tank and pay with a creditcard.

But the Esso has a shop with staff, 24/7 .

What do the supermarkets do every day?

<u>They make sales and profits.
Every day !</u>

What does the Esso do every day and night?

The Esso makes sales day and night,
every day.
<u>So the Esso makes profits,
every day and night of the year</u>

The supermarkets and the Esso are successful
because they realize sales every day
and thus make profits every day.

The Ultimate Winning Strategy for entrepreneurs is making profits every day.

Make a profit every day of the year.

You do that by selling every day,
and by daily closing sales.

Your advantage over your competition

If you sell every day & make profits every day,
do you than have an advantage over companies
who only make profits 5 days a week?

Example 1 from real life

I have been selling from Monday, September 18, 2017
untill Wednesday, September 27, 2017,
10 days in a row,
and made 22 sales in total.

So every day I made sales & I made profits everyday.

That is the Ultimate Winning Strategy for entrepreneurs in action.
(in the real life of running your business)

Well if we are honest,
then we know that the transaction value
of sets of greeting cards is modest.
And therefore the profit per sale is also.

But do not be turned off by those numbers ...
You will soon receive a real life example from someone who
made 1 million.

This was to make you understand the successful Concept
of the Ultimate Winning Strategy for entrepreneurs
and that you see proven that it works.

You now understand that Concept,
you have seen some examples of companies
applying the Ultimate Winning Strategy.
You have seen a real life example
from me I have proven to you that it works.

And you are 100% assured that the Ultimate Winning Strategy works.

People do not need greeting cards
like they need food and drinks,
but they bought every day
and I made profits every day.

So it does not matter what kind of product or service you sell.

<u>The Ultimate Winning Strategy also works for you.</u>

Next step

You understand the Ultimate Winning Strategy for entrepreneurs,
and you know it works.

So now you are going to do it.

You are going to implement it.

I'm not asking you to work 7 days a week,
although you should do it once.
(That will boost your confidence)

You can sell from Monday to Friday &
hire someone who sells for you
from Saturday to Monday (a part-timer)

Then you will already have
sales every day and profits every day.

If I can do it alone,
then you can certainly do it with 2 people!

Are there any other ways how you can
make sales everyday & profits ever day?

Consider, think and find 20 ways,
with which you can make sales everyday

and therefore make profits everyday.

Write them down.

1 Hire a salesperson
2 Create a team of salespeople
3
4
5
6
7
8
9
10
11
12
13
14
15
16
17
18
19
20

Example 2 from real life

Go to www.youtube.nl
and watch the video of Walter Bergeron,
GKIC marketer of the year.

The video lasts about half an hour.

Pay close attention when he says: that means also on saturdays and sundays.

(that he was selling 7 days a week and
making profits every day)

Have you seen
what the Ultimate Winning Strategy for entrepreneurs
can do for you?

Go to work,
go out selling every day & making profits every day.

Apply your 20 ways,
give your sales a boost,
make lots of profits.
Every day of the year.

I wish you a lot of succes.

P.S. If you have liked this book and got good value from it,
than would you be so kind
to recommend it to people that you know.
So that it also helps them forward.
Thank you.

Road to riches, episode 1

hello

how are you today ?

My name is Jasmin Hajro, I was born on july 6th 1985 in Bosnia,

in the war there ,we fled to the Netherlands, where we still live...

In 2015 I hade failed with my first business and was without work and money..

I would visit lots of companies with my resumee and ask for work..

One day I visited about 100 companies , I did't find work...

My sister who was working in door to door sales, said : that's a terry...

In the sales profession, the terry is the amount of people that you have to speak to in one day, that could be 100 addresses...

She and her boyfriend gave me some sales training and an opportunity to sell packages of greetingcards , door to door.

I went to Arnhem (which is a city nearby) and at the chamber of commerce

I started my 2nd company : Hajro

The selling of greetingcards would be good training , so that I eventually could sell to people , the shifting of their utility provider (to save money on gas and electricity)....

So I attented the sales training and one day I asked what the worst thing was that happened in their sales career, it was a doorslam…

I thought I could handle that…and with a little bit of salestraining, my sales presentation written on a piece of paper and a bag full of packages of greetingcards, without being completely ready for the job…

on my own initiative I went out in our neighbourhood and started knocking on doors and selling packages of greetingcards…

In a package there are 5 greetingcards and 5 envelopes and I would sell a package for 5 euros….

Then I found my first customer and then anotherr and then another,

5 years later my business : Hajro (the books & greetingcards company) still exists….I am still going door to door, selling packages of greetingcards.

the Dutch website is www.hajro.be

the english website is www.hajro-international.webnode.nl

the online store is at www.hajroradnja.jouwweb.nl

I have been writing in journals for more than 10 years, a few years ago I decided to publish my writings in books with selfpublishing company's like kobo.com , lulu.com and Amazon's kdp...

Since then I have written and selfpublished more than 45 booklets,

some of them you can read for free, here at medium....

My author website is www.jasminhajro6.webnode.nl

In watching successfull people, watching their videos, reading their books...

you just see a successfull person after 20 or 30 years of hard work....

not often do you see, how they started and earned the first 100 dollars or euros with their business....how they tried things and kept on fighting...

untill now, where they are very successfull....

(Except for maybe in some books or biographies)...

I haven't encountered it often...

And that is what this "Road to riches, episodes" are about...

Starting with nothing, starting a business, earning your first 100 dollars or euros, reinvesting, keeping on selling, and so on untill you reach greater levels of success....

Maybe it's the perspective or the story that is missing out there...

or that isn't told often enough....

To see how it is and goes in reality...not in theory...

So in september 2015 I started my 2nd business, that sells packages of greetingcards, door to door...I got some sales training and went out selling in our neighbourhood....I started to make sales....

I did try some things,...like building an online store

with different kinds of packages of greetingcards and other Hajro labeled products....and then I would write a flyer and have it printed a couple of thousand times... and I would deliver my flyer to hundreds of mailboxes...

inviting the people to my companys website and online store...

and then nobody would order anything....

Then I couldn't pay the website on time and someone bought the webadress,

so I had to make a new website....

That is one of the greetingcards that I would buy in bulk from Belgium,

and package and resell...this one is for birthdays.....

In 2016 I earned on monthly average of E 140,- euros

I was still living with my mother., who paid the rent and the other living expenses....

In 2017 I averaged monthly E 108,- euros in profits

In 2018 I averaged monthly E 261,- euros in profits...

Maybe I am a slow learner....

You don't encounter these kind of numbers out there, do you ???

In 2019 I averaged monthly 281,- euros in profits Plus I earned at a job where I worked for 3 months E 2414,69 euros

Last year in 2020 I averaged monthly E 487,- euros in profits Plus I received E 2678,16 in subsidy from the government....

In my worst month I sold 200 greetingcards, in my best month I sold more than 700 greetingcards for 1 euro a piece.....

My company has a new website and new online store by now...

I have also written about 10 booklets last year.

Now in 2021 we are in lockdown...

I have received subsidy from the government of E650 euros a month.,

and I will continue to receive it untill the revenue from my business exceeds that amount a couple of months in a row....

I have been tasered, drugged, had a box of greetingcards been stolen from me...

tired and exhausted.....But I am still standing and so is my business...

While in lockdown, only essential companys are open , like the supermarkets and pharmacies, who sell essential products, like food and medicine...

I started selling loafs of bread and bottles of carbon water,

and I managed to make some sales offline, with door to door selling...

while being in national lockdown...

I have also ordered flyers for my business and author website

and I am delivering those to peoples mailboxes and doing offline marketing....

As you can imagine my debts have accumulated over the years,

and it sucks when you can't pay the dentist....

Now that I am earning more and receiving more, I am paying everybody back...

It's still a struggle...I also still struggle with getting up early (now I have medicine for that)

I do have a disabilty , I damaged my brain a little bit when I was younger by drinking too much and using too much drugs (I also have medicine for that)

Maybe Brian Tracey says it best :"In business everything cost twice as much and takes twice the amount of time, than yu thought it would"

By now I also have designed myself some of our greetingcards, liike the one below

That is in short how my business adventure developed,

which we call "Road to riches"

Road to riches, episode 2

hello,

how are you today ?

It is now 10 january 2021,

we still have 10 days of lockdown to go…

I wanted to Tweet : I sold loafs of bread and bottles of carbon water in this lockdown, my mama bought 2 little birds…while we have a cat as a pet…

and I was rejected for a writing job, by an algorhytm….

Life is at it's weirdest…

But I didn't tweet it…

I have social media accounts…I have ''shared'' and posted news, quotes, sayings, messages, questions and so on…over the years…

Every time I write a new book, I ''social share'' it…

And every time I translate a dutch book of mine, into english, I also ''social share'' it....

I have a company page for my company Hajro at Facebook...

I also have the page ''Jasmin Hajro books and fans'' for my readers,

where I share updates about my books and also my videos...

I don't think social media got me any customers or sales,

not 1 !!!

In december I have earned 0,01 cent at Medium for my stories...

(I am not a long time on medium, maybe just 1 year)

But it's more than I have earned with my social media channels...

Perhaps I should have done some advertising on social media,

(I didn't have the money for that)

I also know that it's hard to measure....

If I deliver 1000 flyers, I will see in my author website dashboard, how many people have visited my author website...

If I have 1000 likes or shares on social media, I don't know

how many will visit...

I am not a social media expert, and I haven't figured out how to make it (social media)work for my business....

From my prefessional experience as a business owner, in the last 5 years

it seems like a waste of time and energy....

Maybe that is not the most popular opinion, but it is my personal experience...

That is a unique greetingcards, that I have designed...

I have sold about 200 of those, door to door in packages of 5 greetingcards.

Yesterday I visited my sister and her kids in town Wehl,

I went out selling and sold 4 bottles of carbon water along with a package of greetingcards, in lockdown time.

But water is essential, so I can continue to do business...

Today I also went out selling door to door, I sold 2 bottles of carbon water and 2 packages of greetingcards....

The last time I delivered flyers, they were partially about some of my books,

and I got a bump in booksales then...

I think I will stick to what works in my business,

selling door to door of food and non food products,

writing more books and perhaps a few stories at medium...

and delivering flyers offline to peoples mailboxes...

I will make a video or 2 once in a while....

(If I think about it, that is how I got to the books that I bought

by Brian Tracey, Jim Rohn, Dan S. Kennedy and Les Brown.

By first watching some of their videos on youtube).

Maybe you"ll get some value from these "Road to riches episodes"

maybe they will only give you a perspective on how it is in reality

to have your own business and be an entrepreneur...

Thank you for reading....

If you enjoy my stories at medium, you will probably enjoy my books,

you can find them
at www.jasminhajro6.webnode.nl

(there I give away my first 10 booklets for free, so it's worth a visit)

Till next time...

Kind regards,

Jasmin Hajro

I hope I have given you insight

in how it is really

in reality,

when you start your own business…

And hopefully

You are encouraged to start your own business and make it a big success….

Even if it takes for you to First

get experience in door to door selling,

before you start it…

I would suggest

1 get experience in door to door selling

2 learn marketing

3 study and practise copywriting

and save money,

you'll always need it !

A few things have changed since I wrote this book…
I am still a business owner,
my company is still Hajro,
I still sell packages of greetingcards, door to door…
even in national lockdown…

My companys website is www.hajro.be
the english website is
www.hajro-international.webnode.nl
our online store is at
www.hajroradnja.jouwweb.nl

my author website is
www.jasminhajro6.webnode.nl

I wish for you the best of life and much success.
Kind regards,
Jasmin Hajro

More books by Jasmin Hajro :

My bibliography....the books that I have written....

(there are more than 43 titles plus the translations plus the boxsets, so I will only name my english titles)

Build Your Fortune

Moneymaker

Recipe For Happiness

the Lifebuoy For Banks "Loyal Banking"

the Ultimate Winning Strategy, for entrepreneurs (which is for salespeople & businessowners too)

Poems, jokes and book

Victory 1

Victory 2

Always employment & always money in your pocket, everyday.

Things You Don't Want To Know.

Challenges in having your own business, in real life.

how to Grow your money & Build a good retirement in 2 hours per month, for moms, dads, career women and busy people .

Overcoming tough times.

Secrets of writing and selling books.

Double your profits.

Double your profits, extended.

Triumph 1 (boxset)

Triumph 2 (boxset)

Victorious series (boxset)

Through the crisis

Victory 3

My story

My little masterpiece

Victory 4

I don't feel like writing, says the author

Hackers are scouts

Being real and true: in times of fake and pretend

100 % sales rule

Quotes for success

Entrepreneurship course

3

(If you click on them a new window will open, at Lulu, where you learn more about the book

and where you can buy it as paperback or ebook.

If the link doesn't work click here

All my titles are there, but you can search the one that you want..

" I have good experiences ordering at Lulu")

Only available at Amazon and free with Kindle Unlimited are my books :

Lifechanging quotes

the Jasmin Hajro lifestory(which includes Victory 1,2,3,4)

Controversial

This is how you get rich: passively

200 % sales rule

Visit my author website and get 10 free books at
www.jasminhajro6.webnode.nl

Note :

Over the years a few websites have changed....
My author website is now and will always be at
www.jasminhajro6.webnode.nl

You get 10 free books if you visit me there..

Thank you for choosing one of my books to read.

Hopefully you are willing to rate it 4 or 5 startingand give it a positive review.

Thank you so much
for your effort.

I will continue to sell greetingcards
and write more books
untill retirement,
so more good stuff will be available
at my Author website,
www.jasminhajro6.webnode.nl
make sure that you visit it
every year or
more often than that.

Kind regards,
Jasmin Hajro
P.S. I hope this book helps you to change your life..

www.ingramcontent.com/pod-product-compliance
Lightning Source LLC
Chambersburg PA
CBHW080520220526
45465CB00006B/2549